Claire Llewellyn

Story illustrated by
Steve May

Heineman

Before Reading

In this story

 Jed Jed's mum

 The piranha

Tricky words

- note
- teeth
- jumped
- plaster
- finger
- again
- nose
- why

> Introduce these tricky words and help the reader when they come across them later!

Story starter

Jed's mum is a vet. She looks after sick animals. Sometimes she keeps an animal overnight at her home. One day, Mum had to go out. She left a note for Jed asking him to feed the piranha.

Jed
and the
Piranha

Jed looked at the note.

Jed looked at the fish.

The fish had lots and lots of teeth.

Jed fed the fish.

The fish jumped up
and bit Jed.

Jed put a plaster on his finger.

7

Jed fed the fish again.

The fish jumped up again and bit Jed on the nose.

Jed put a plaster on his nose.

Jed was fed up.
He looked at the fish.

Then he got a plaster.

What do you think
Jed is going to do?

Mum got back and looked at Jed.

"Why have you got a plaster on your nose?" said Mum.

Then Mum looked at the fish.

"And why has the fish got a plaster on its nose?"

Quiz

Text Detective

- Why was Jed fed up?
- Do you think Mum will think Jed has done the right thing?

Word Detective

- Phonic Focus: Final letter sounds
  Page 6: Find a word that ends with the phoneme 'd'.
- Page 8: Find a word that means 'one more time'.
- Page 12: Find a word ending 'ed'.

Super Speller

Read these words:

and   fed   bit

Now try to spell them!

HA! HA! HA!

Q What fish only comes out at night?

A A star fish!

Find out about

- Dangerous animals that live in water

Tricky words

- dangerous
- sharp
- teeth
- strong
- jaws
- tail
- sting
- most

Introduce these tricky words and help the reader when they come across them later!

Text starter

Many dangerous animals like piranhas, killer whales, stingrays and sharks live in water. Some of them are small but they have sharp teeth. Some are big and have strong jaws or a dangerous sting.

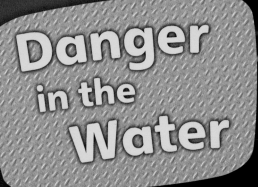

Danger in the Water

This fish is dangerous.
It is not big but it has
sharp teeth.

What is it?

A piranha's teeth are as sharp as a razor!

It is a piranha!

Piranhas live in rivers.
They are very dangerous.

This animal has big strong jaws and sharp teeth.

What is it?

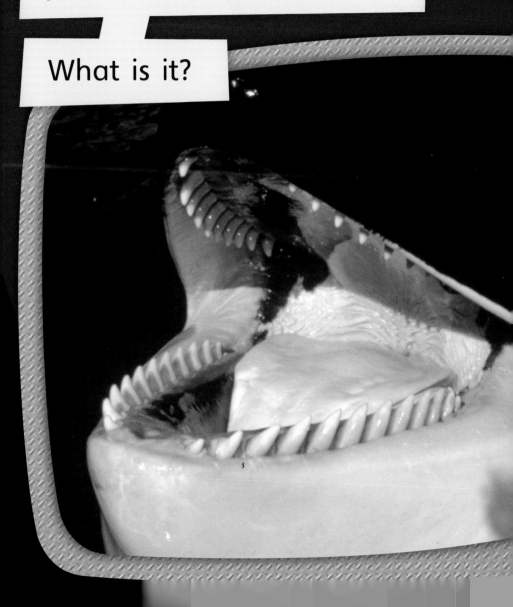

It is a killer whale!

Killer whales live in the sea but they are not fish.

Killer whales are mammals.

This fish lives in the sea.
Its tail has a sting in it.

What is it?

It is a stingray!

A stingray has a dangerous sting.

This fish is a killer.
It has big strong jaws
and sharp teeth.

What is it?

It is a great white shark!

Great white sharks are the most dangerous fish in the sea.

Quiz

Text Detective

- Why is the piranha so dangerous?
- Which animal do you think is the most scary? Why?

Word Detective

- **Phonic Focus:** Final letter sounds
  Page 19: Find a word that ends with the phoneme 'l'.
- Page 17: Can you find a word that means 'powerful'?
- Page 19: Find a word to rhyme with 'bring'.

Super Speller

Read these words:

is   big   they

Now try to spell them!

HA! HA! HA!

Q Why are fish easy to weigh?

A They have their own scales!

24